Finding Peace with Jesus

Prayers & Thoughts

by Fr Seán Finnegan

All booklets are published thanks to the generous support of the members of the Catholic Truth Society

CATHOLIC TRUTH SOCIETY
PUBLISHERS TO THE HOLY SEE

Contents

My Family 5

On Your Own 9

When Things Get Tough 13

Which Path To Choose 17

True Friendship 21

True Happiness 25

The Christian Faith offers us something genuinely new each day.

Christ himself offers us peace in the face of anxiety, life in the face of death, forgiveness in the face of selfishness and honest answers to our heartfelt questions.

Reader please note that references to the *Compendium of the Catechism of the Catholic Church* are identified by paragraph, eg: (c. 337).

My Family

———————

*E*ven if our physical family has, for one reason or another, been taken from us, families are still something familiar to most of us. Human beings are meant to belong to each other. We wither when cut off from others.

Catholics see the family as being one of the most important building blocks of society - where the family is protected, there society can flourish most fruitfully. Where it is not supported, then society itself becomes more and more dysfunctional.

What the Bible says

*W*hen the time had fully come, God sent forth his Son, born of woman, born under the law, to redeem those who were under the law, so that we might receive adoption as sons. And because you are sons, God has sent the Spirit of his Son into our hearts, crying, "Abba! Father!" So through God you are no longer a slave but a son, and if a son then an heir. (*Galatians* 4:1-7)

Reflection

Here, then, we have the ideal of marriage. It should be complete dedication to the other person, without regard to one's own happiness, in the confidence that the other is doing the same thing. This sort of love is always fruitful; it gives rise to the Holy Spirit. True love goes far beyond those who live in its ambit and touches all who come into contact with it. "He who loses his life will find it." (*Luke* 17:33)

What others say

The great danger for family life, in the midst of any society whose idols are pleasure, comfort and independence, lies in the fact that people close their hearts and become selfish. (*Pope John Paul II*)

What the Church Says

What is the plan of God regarding man and woman?

God who is love and who created man and woman for love has called them to love. By creating man and woman he called them to an intimate communion of life and of love in marriage: "So that they are no longer two, but one flesh" (*Matthew* 19:6). God said to them in blessing "Be fruitful and multiply" (*Genesis* 1:28). (c. 337)

A sincere prayer

Lord God, I recognize that you have called me to belong to a wider family of your people in a special way. I ask you to help me steer away from a preoccupation with my own comfort. Help me find myself in others, that my love may be fruitful and tend to your glory and my salvation. Through Christ our Lord.

On Your Own

There is being alone, and there is being lonely. The two are rarely the same thing. I can be on my own without a care in the world, and I can be in a crowd and horribly lonely. The difference is knowing that somebody cares, even if they aren't near me.

What the Bible says

My God, my God, why have you forsaken me?
Why are you so far from saving me,
so far from the words of my groaning?
O my God, I cry out by day,
but you do not answer, by night, and am not silent...
In you our fathers put their trust;
they trusted and you delivered them.
They cried to you and were saved;
in you they trusted and were not disappointed.

But you, O Lord, be not far off;
O my Strength, come quickly to help me. (*Psalm* 22)

Reflection

Human beings are made for love, both giving love and receiving love. But it is true that on the whole we will only be offered love if we have given it in the first place, and the more we withdraw, the more others will withdraw from us. It is also worth remembering that there is somebody who will never abandon us: God. And he, of course knows exactly what is going on in our minds, and what we are feeling. He knows what abandonment is - the psalm written above was one he quoted when on the cross. That this is why he gave us the sacrament of the Eucharist, to bind us closely to himself, and the sacrament of Penance to heal any damage between us.

What others say

When you look at the crucifix, you understand how much Jesus loved you. When you look at the Sacred Host, you understand how much Jesus loves you now. (*Blessed Mother Teresa of Calcutta*)

What the Church says

In what way does God reveal that he is love?

God revealed himself to Israel as the One who has a stronger love than that of parents for their children or of husbands and wives for their spouses. God in himself "is love" (1 *John* 4:8.16), who gives himself completely and gratuitously, who "so loved the world that he gave his only Son so that the world might be saved through him" (*John* 3:16-17). By sending his Son and the Holy Spirit, God reveals that he himself is an eternal exchange of love. (c. 42)

A sincere prayer

Dear Father, I know that I am never truly alone because you are always there to watch over me and care for me. Help me to feel your presence more keenly, to know the warmth of your love that I may share it with others.

When Things Get Tough

Sometimes we can look at others who seem to have everything; looks, wealth, faith, friends, family, intelligence, and so much besides. It sometimes seems that God has short-changed us in some way, put us at a disadvantage before others. We know in our hearts that this isn't true, but when things get tough, it isn't always easy to remember it.

What the Bible says

If God is for us, who is against us? He who did not spare his own Son but gave him up for us all, will he not also give us all things with him?... Who shall separate us from the love of Christ? Shall tribulation, or distress, or persecution, or famine, or nakedness, or peril, or sword?... No, in all these things we are more than conquerors through him who loved us. For I am sure that neither death, nor life, nor angels, nor principalities, nor things present, nor things to come, nor powers, nor height, nor depth, nor anything else in all creation, will be able to separate us from the love of God in Christ Jesus our Lord. (*Romans* 8:31-39)

Reflection

Life does have its challenges; even those golden people who seem blessed in every possible way have to carry the cross in some way or other. It is a fact of life, and a fruit of sin; not necessarily our own personal sin, but the general sinfulness of humanity. This is a consequence of a world that rejects God; God has accepted our choice, and respects the decisions which we have made.

However, in Christ, he has done something wonderful. He has shown us that suffering, which is the just penalty for sin, can also be the way out. By accepting the things that happen to us generously from the hand of God, they become redemptive. That is why Christ suffered and was raised from the dead. If we offer our sufferings with his, and put our faith in his saving death, then we shall share his resurrection.

What others say

If God causes you to suffer much, it is a sign that he has great designs for you and that he certainly intends to make you a saint. (*St Ignatius of Loyola*)

What the Church says

How do we collaborate with divine Providence?

While respecting our freedom, God asks us to cooperate with him and gives us the ability to do so through actions, prayers and sufferings, thus awakening in us the desire "to will and to work for his good pleasure" (*Philippians* 2:13). (c. 56)

A sincere prayer

Give me thy grace, Good God, to set the world at nought, to set my mind fast upon thee and not to hang upon the words of men's mouths, to be content to be solitary, not to long for worldly company, little by little utterly to cast off the world, and rid my mind of all besides thee,... Lord, give me patience in tribulation and grace in everything to conform my will to thine, that I may truly say, 'thy will be done on earth as it is in heaven.' The things, good Lord, that I pray for, give me grace to labour for. Amen. (*St Thomas More*)

Which Path To Choose

Choices face us all day, every day. Shall I eat this, or that? Shall I say this to somebody or not? Some choices are morally neutral; nobody gets hurt either way. Others are not. As Christians, we are called to do good and avoid evil, but sometimes it seems as if we are caught in a trap and compelled to a course of action that we would rather not do.

What the Bible says

I do not do the good I want, but the evil I do not want is what I do. (*Romans* 7:19)

Listen Israel! The Lord your God is the only one. You shall love the Lord your God with all your heart, with all your mind and with all your strength and you shall love your neighbour as yourself. Do this and you shall live forever. (*Deuteronomy* 6)

Reflection

*H*uman freedom consists in our ability to act in accord with our nature, which is *both* spiritual *and* physical. We start from understanding principles with our minds, and then applying them to ourselves with our wills. This can be tough, because we know only too well that we are fallen, that our souls and bodies don't work terribly efficiently, and it takes a lot of willpower, sometimes, to do the right thing. And yet, the more we do the right thing, the more we become free. We find ourselves and are able to really choose our actions in the future, and not be simply dragged along by our disordered instincts.

We find these principles in the scriptures and in the teaching of the Church. It is part of the reason that the Church is here, to help us find the way to heaven by ordering ourselves towards that end. It is to help us become free.

What others say

*L*ead, kindly Light, amid th'encircling gloom,
lead thou me on!
The night is dark, and I am far from home;
lead thou me on!

Keep thou my feet; I do not ask to see
the distant scene; one step enough for me.
(*Cardinal John Henry Newman*)

What the Church says

What is freedom?

Freedom is the power given by God to act or not to act, to do this or to do that, and so to perform deliberate actions on one's own responsibility. Freedom characterizes properly human acts. The more one does what is good, the freer one becomes. Freedom attains its proper perfection when it is directed toward God, the highest good and our beatitude. Freedom implies also the possibility of choosing between good and evil. The choice of evil is an abuse of freedom and leads to the slavery of sin. (c. 363)

A sincere prayer

Almighty God, grant us the sight and clear wisdom to see what needs to be done, and the courage to do it. Through Christ our Lord. Amen.

True Friendship

Some have said that friendship is the most important of the human relationships that we experience. For many, if not most, married people, it is friendship that keeps the relationship steady. Friendship should not be jealous or exclusive; we can have many friends, all with different points where they touch our lives, but the best are those with whom we can be ourselves without fear of rejection or condemnation.

What the Bible says

Let love be genuine; hate what is evil, hold fast to what is good; love one another with brotherly affection; outdo one another in showing honour. Never flag in zeal, be aglow with the Spirit, serve the Lord. Rejoice in your hope, be patient in tribulation, be constant in prayer. Contribute to the needs of the saints, practice hospitality.

Bless those who persecute you; bless and do not curse them. Rejoice with those who rejoice, weep with those who weep. Live in harmony with one another; do not be haughty, but associate with the lowly; never be conceited. Repay no one evil for evil, but take thought for what is noble in the sight of all. If possible, so far as it depends upon you, live peaceably with all. (*Romans* 12:9-18)

Reflection

*F*riendships rarely just happen to us; we have to meet them half way and remember that they are as much about giving as receiving and, like all relationships, they can wither and die if they are not tended.

Friendship is about going out from yourself and finding yourself in another; in this way it can be said to be a profoundly Christian thing. If you take a real interest in others, if you want to hear about them more than you want to tell them about yourself, then you will start finding friends straight away. It is as simple as that.

What others say

*T*here is nothing on this earth more to be prized than true friendship. (*Saint Thomas Aquinas*)

What the Church says

What is contemplative prayer?

Contemplative prayer is a simple gaze upon God in silence and love. It is a gift of God, a moment of pure faith during which the one praying seeks Christ, surrenders himself to the loving will of the Father, and places his being under the action of the Holy Spirit. Saint Teresa of Avila defines contemplative prayer as the intimate sharing of friendship, "in which time is frequently taken to be alone with God who we know loves us." (c. 571)

A sincere prayer

*D*ear Lord, give me your own gift of friendship. Help me to set myself aside; to listen to others more than to myself, to be a tower of strength to those I love when they are in trouble, to give without counting the cost. Dear Lord, make me like you.

True Happiness

Human beings are made for happiness, and the fact that we spend a lot of the time unhappy is a real violation of our true nature. The trouble is that we look for it in the wrong place; seeking to take happiness from the world around us, whereas anybody who is truly happy will tell you that happiness comes from making others happy. Happiness is found in moving outwards, not inwards.

What the Bible says

Blessed are you when men revile you and persecute you and utter all kinds of evil against you falsely on my account. Rejoice and be glad, for your reward is great in heaven, for so men persecuted the prophets who were before you. (*Matthew* 5)

Reflection

It is the ultimate human question: how can I become happy? We can see that our Lord tells us that the sorts of things that will make us happy are just the opposite to what one might have supposed. Our home, our happiness lies ultimately in heaven, and we must not expect to find this world ~~truly~~ *completely* satisfying. Indeed often it will crucify us, as it crucified the Lord. But, since we already live in the Kingdom of God, we can expect to find its blessings even now if we look, and the more we conform our lives to the Kingdom, then the happier we will be.

What others say

Sorrows and suffering can be a paradise if I suffer with God. On the other hand, the greatest pleasure in the world would be like hell to me, if I tasted it apart from Jesus. (*Brother Lawrence*)

What the Church says

Why does man have a desire for God?

God himself, in creating man in his own image, has written upon his heart the desire to see him. Even if this desire is often ignored, God never ceases to draw man to himself because only in God will he find and live the fullness of truth and happiness for which he never stops searching. By nature and by vocation, therefore, man is a religious being, capable of entering into communion with God. This intimate and vital bond with God confers on man his fundamental dignity. (c. 1)

A sincere prayer

Lord, help me to seek happiness in your will, and in the good of my neighbour. Take away from me all self-centred pleasures that lead me away from your presence and your love. Grant me your peace that the world cannot give.

Informative Catholic Reading

We hope that you have enjoyed reading this booklet.

If you would like to find out more about CTS booklets - we'll send you our free information pack and catalogue.

Please send us your details:

Name ....

Address ....

....

....

Postcode ....

Telephone..

Email ....

Send to: CTS, 40-46 Harleyford Road,
            Vauxhall, London
            SE11 5AY

Tel: 020 7640 0042
Fax: 020 7640 0046
Email: info@cts-online.org.uk